22.2.29.

SBN 531–00052–4

Library of Congress Catalog Card Number: 62-9235
Printed in the United States of America
by The Moffa Press, Inc.

LET'S FIND OUT ABOUT

WATER

by

MARTHA and CHARLES SHAPP

Pictures by Richard Mayhew

FRANKLIN WATTS, INC.
575 Lexington Avenue, New York 22

Everybody and everything needs water.
You need water.

Your pets need water.

All animals need water.
Jungle animals need water.

Farm animals need water.

All plants need water.
Plants in the garden need water.

Plants on the farm need water.

Water is needed for washing.
You need water to wash yourself . . .

. . . and to wash your dog.

Water is used to wash everything – from dishes . . .

. . . to streets.

Water is needed to put out fires.

Where does all the water come from?
It comes from the clouds.

Some of the rain sinks into the ground.
Many people get water from under the ground.

Some rain water comes down the mountains in streams.

The streams come together to make lakes.

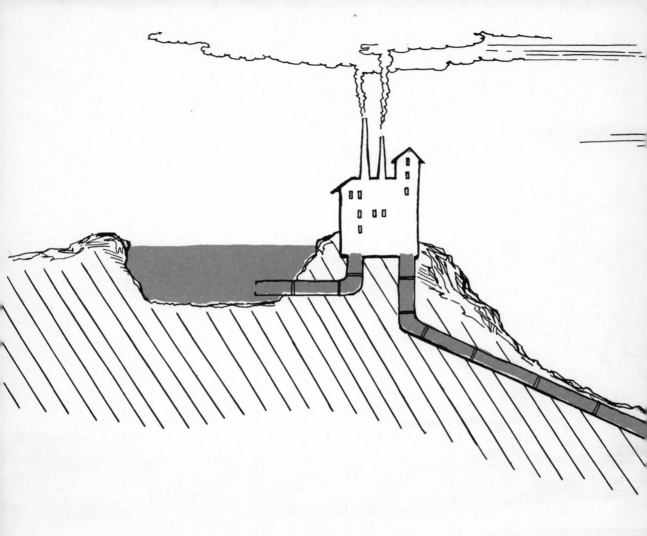

Many people get water from these lakes.
The water is piped from the lakes.

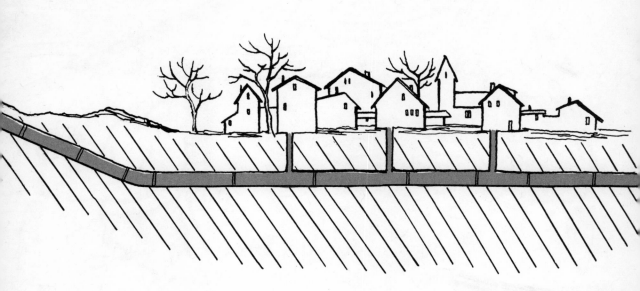

You can have fun with water.

Swimming is fun.

Fishing is fun.

Water can do many things that seem almost like magic.

It can hold up many things.

A big ship can float in water.

Some things cannot float.
Put a penny into some water.

The penny sinks.

Water can change itself.
When water gets very cold, it becomes ice.

When water gets very hot, it becomes steam.

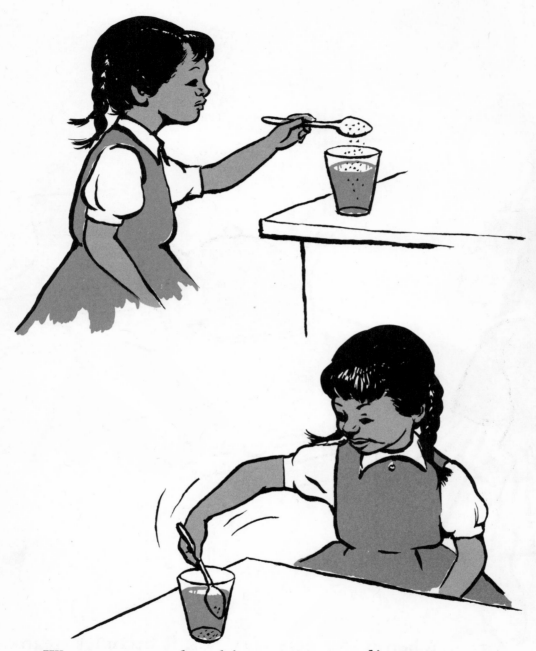

Water can make things seem to disappear.
Put some sugar into water.
Stir the water.

The sugar seems to have disappeared.
Taste the water.
Is the sugar there?

Water can disappear into the air.
Rain makes the street wet.

The rain stops.
Soon the street is dry.
The water has disappeared into the air.

Mother hangs wet clothes out in the air.

Soon the clothes are dry. The water in the
clothes has disappeared into the air.

Water that disappears into the air becomes clouds.

Out of the clouds comes the rain that brings the water.

VOCABULARY LIST (99 words)

a	get(s)	rain
air	ground	
all		seem
almost	hangs	ship
and	has	sink
animals	have	some
are	hold	soon
	hot	steam
becomes		stir
big	ice	stops
brings	in	streams
	into	streets
can	is	sugar
cannot	it	swimming
change	itself	
clothes		taste
clouds	jungle	that
cold		the
come(s)	lake(s)	there
	like	these
disappear(ed)		things
dishes	magic	to
do	make(s)	together
does	many	
dog	mother	under
down	mountains	up
dry		used
	need(s) (ed)	
everybody		very
everything	of	
	on	wash(ing)
farm	out	water
fires		wet
fishing	penny	when
float	people	where
for	pets	with
from	piped	
fun	plants	you
	put	your
garden		yourself

42